Using drugs B1

Crush a B1 pill and then mix it in the flower arrangement. B1 pills will help the flower branches absorb water faster. However, this method is only effective with hard-bodied flowers such as roses, chrysanthemums, hydrangeas...

How to keep flowers fresh for a long time with apple cider vinegar

Everyone wants to keep their flowers fresh for a long time in a vase. And there are some pretty good methods for doing this. One of the ways to keep flowers from wilting is to mix 2 tablespoons of apple cider vinegar and 2 tablespoons of sugar into the water before arranging the flowers. Remember to change the water (with vinegar and sugar added, of course) every day to increase the "life" of your flowers.

How to keep flowers fresh for a long time with
Apple Cider Vinegar
White sugar

The most commonly used way to arrange flowers without rot is to make your own flower preservative from white sugar. Dissolve 3 tablespoons of sugar and 2 tablespoons of white vinegar in each quart of warm water. When you pour this solution into the jar make sure the stem is covered with 7-10cm of water.

Sugar nourishes plants, accelerates photosynthesis; while vinegar inhibits the growth of bacteria. You will be surprised that after a long time, the flowers are still fresh with this way to keep them fresh for a long time.

CONTENTS

Arrange Red Lilies

Supplies needed:

- 10 branches of yellow daisies
- 10 branches of red lily
- 2 branches of orchid leaves
- 5 branches of betel leaves
- 5 branches of spotted bamboo leaves
- Large glass flower vase
- Flower scissors
- Duct tape

How to arrange red lilies:

Step 1 Pour water into the jar

First, you fill the vase with water about ⅔ height, then crush 1-2 aspirin pills and dissolve in water, this will help the flowers last longer.

Step 2 Glue tape

Next, you use clear tape to stick the mouth of the vase in the shape of a checkerboard, this will help the flowers stand more firmly when plugged in and distribute more evenly.

Step 3 Pruning flower branches

You use scissors to cross cut the branches of red lilies, yellow daisies to increase the surface area for water absorption for flowers. The flower spikes should be approximately the same height and more than 2 or 2.5 times the height of the vase.

Step 4 Insert the red lily

Next, you stick each stem of the red lily into the vase so that they are facing the same direction. The distance between the flower branches should be evenly aligned and form a propeller shape.

Step 5 Plant yellow daisies

Then, you plug each chrysanthemum branch alternately with the previously plugged red lily. Should be arranged so that the chrysanthemum branches are lower and closer to the mouth of the vase than the lily.

Step 6 Insert orchid leaves, betel leaves, spotted bamboo leaves

In the last step, you stick the orchid leaves in the middle, alternating with the flower branches and make the leaves radiating. Then attach the betel leaves, spotted bamboo leaves around the mouth of the vase to cover the tape, the base and the stem of the flower branch.

Finished products:

So with just 6 very simple steps, you have yourself a vase of red lilies combined with the yellow color of chrysanthemums filled with Tet atmosphere for your family.

Reveal some tips when arranging flowers:

When choosing flowers, you should choose flowers with large, strong and sturdy stems. Leaves should be bright green, have a certain shine and shine.

If you want to arrange a flower with a slightly curved shape, when planting, just use your hand to gently bend at the top of the flower until the desired curvature is achieved.

When you want to arrange a traditional flower arrangement in a tall vase, you should cross the flower stalk to spread the flower wide. The order of plugging will be from the outer ring to the inside, the outer branches plug shallower than the inner branches.

Flowers for the altar should not be combined with too many colors, usually only 2-3 colors should be used that can harmoniously complement each other.

Flowers for the altar should not be spread out to the sides because it may hide the image of the deceased. Instead, it should be plugged forward or upwards.

Arrange Gladiolus Flowers

Materials:

Flowers to arrange: how to arrange gladiolus flowers on Tet holiday
- 19 gladiolus branches.

You will notice that even the crooked gladiolus branches do not need to be removed. You just need to pay attention to choose the lowest and most inclined position to plug so that the flower tops are bent in the direction straight up. If the flower branches are too crooked, you can use scissors to press the branches, remove the crooked tops and keep the lower flower branches as normal.
- 12 sprigs of royal flowers
- 8 fern leaves in a gladiolus flower arrangement on Tet holiday
- Tall glass flower vase how to arrange gladiolus flowers on Tet holiday
- Styrofoam how to arrange grateful flowers on Tet holiday
- Scissors cut flower branches

How to arrange gladiolus flowers:

Step 1: Soak the sponge to absorb the water evenly and then put it in a glass jar (2/3 of the sponge is in the jar, the remaining 1/3 is on the top of the jar).
Step 2: Insert gladiolus flowers into the foam, face the flowers forward, adjust the low height to form a fan shape.

How to bend gladiolus: Before placing the flowers in the foam, use your hand to slightly bend the part near the top so that the flower will naturally bend the next day in the direction you want.

Step 3: Stick the fern leaves around, low close to the mouth of the jar and face forward to cover the sponge in the way of arranging gladiolus flowers on Tet holiday or to the altar.

Step 4: Finally, arrange the cycad flowers in the middle of the fern and gladiolus. Note that the cycads will be taller than the fern leaves and also face forward.

With the way of arranging gladiolus flowers on Tet holiday, you have got a vase of flowers to display on the ancestral altar or living room on Tet that will make your home space full of spring colors.

In this flowerpot, you can still see that there are still some of the lowest flower branches that are slightly crooked when they have just been plugged into the vase without being removed.

Don't worry too much, with the newly planted gladiolus, you have slightly bent the part near the top of the flower when you put it, just after 1 night, all the flower branches will slightly bend and reach the top. I don't need to find out what other ways to bend gladiolus flowers do.

Arrange Jasmine Flowers

Ingredient:

- jasmine flower
- vase of flowers
- styrofoam or glue
- scissors
- other flowers or leaves

Making:

Step 1: Fill the cotton vase with water about ⅔ of its height. Then add about 1 aspirin tablet to let it remove all the toxins of the water, helping the flowers stay fresh longer and more beautiful.

Step 2: You can insert foam or glue for the jasmine tree to stand. It helps the flower plant to more evenly distribute the sides. Thanks to that, the vase will look eye-catching and convenient for flower arrangement.

Step 3: Before planting cotton, cut the base of the plant diagonally with a sharp knife or scissors to help the plant easily absorb moisture and stay fresh longer. Choose different long and short branches to create uniqueness for the vase.

Step 4: After arranging jasmine flowers in sufficient quantity, you should insert other colorful flowers such as carnations, daisies, etc. to create a highlight for the vase. If you follow a noble and luxurious style, you do not need to insert extra flowers.

Step 5: You insert mimosa leaves or other auxiliary leaves to help the vase look fuller and more harmonious.

Step 6: After you have inserted the leaves and flowers, you need to choose a reasonable display location. Jasmine flowers are often suitable for display in the living room, dining table, banquet table or altar. Choose a suitable location and have a stable temperature to display your flowers.

Arrange ahlias

Supplies needed:

- Dahlia flowers (young branches and flower buds)
- Flower vase
- Styrofoam flower arrangement

Good tip:

Dahlia flowers, you should choose fresh flowers, have long branches and flower branches must have enough big flowers, flower buds, old leaves, young leaves. In particular, you should choose flowers with even green leaves, not crushed, and flowers, the layers of petals and flower stalks must be long, hard, without bad smell.

For flower vases, you should choose round vases, cylindrical vases or flared vases!

How to arrange dahlia flowers:

Step 1 Shaping the flower arrangement

First, you fill the flower foam with water and choose 4 dahlia branches to plug into the 4 corners of the sponge to shape the flower arrangement.

Note: You should determine the position so that 4 flower branches will be like anchors hooked to the mouth of the vase.

Step 2 Put the flowers in the vase

Once shaped, gently move the flower arrangement foam into the vase. Next, you plug alternately young branches and flower buds around the mouth of the vase.

Then, you plug the remaining dahlia branches in turn in a slanting fashion and alternately with each other, you plug so that the front, back, left, right side are balanced!

Step 3: Finished product

With just a few simple steps, you have a beautiful vase of dahlias with a simple, balanced and very beautiful layout. It seems that the vase of dahlias has made the space here more alive.

yoke to keep dahlia flowers fresh for a long time, hard-stemmed:

When buying flowers, you should immediately put them in a bucket of water (don't let the water cover the cotton) within 30 minutes. This will help provide enough water for the flower parts, helping the flowers stay fresh longer. Adding vinegar to the vase about 1 minute before plugging is one of the ways to help flowers stay fresh for a long time and harden. Because white vinegar combines with water as a catalyst to limit flower wilting.

Adding sugar to the vase will help the flowers stay fresh longer because sugar helps increase the photosynthesis of the flower stems.

Putting a little cold tea in the flower vase is also a way many people use because it will help your flowers stay fresh for 7 days!

Arrange Beautiful And Simple Daisies

How to arrange beautiful and long-lasting star flowers:

Ingredient

- 1 bunch of daisies
- Vase of flowers
- Country
- Drag
- Aspirin (available at drugstores)

How to arrange simple, long-lasting chrysanthemum flowers:

Step 1 After buying, you should put the flowers in a bucket filled with water for about 3-4 hours for the flowers to absorb the cool water again.

Step 2 Must trim all the leaves because the leaves rot very quickly, absorb all the water, making the flowers not fresh, wilt and cover the flowers. The small flower buds that could not bloom were not regretful but had to be removed.

Step 3 Use scissors to cut the base of the flower at an angle of 45 degrees and in an aquatic environment to ensure that the water reaches the flower fastest, without air bubbles.

Step 4 Put 1 aspirin in the flower arrangement, it has the effect of inhibiting the growth of bacteria. Every day, every time you change the water, add a small aspirin.

Step 5 Place the flowers in the vase right after cutting the branches.

Step 6 Should only be dipped in water about 3cm, because chrysanthemum absorbs water through the stem and will rot if submerged. So low water will help prevent this problem from happening, helping plants stay fresh longer.

Tips to keep chrysanthemums fresh longer:

Leave the chrysanthemum flowers in a temperature of about 18-25 degrees. Should avoid places with high temperature, or contact with high temperature objects such as TV, fan heater, on refrigerator, ...

Avoid placing chrysanthemums near ripe fruits or vegetables, because ethylene gas released during the ripening process of vegetables, tubers and fruits causes flowers to wilt faster.

Rinse and change the water in the tank twice a day, this will limit the plant rot and eliminate the habitat of bacteria.

If the base of the stem becomes shriveled or wilted, prune the base slightly to improve water absorption.

Arrange A Low Radial Carnation Vase

The carnation is a beautiful flower grown in cold Mediterranean climates. With its attractive beauty, it is loved by many people. Having a vase of carnations in the office or living room adds to the beauty of your space, bringing a sense of relaxation after stressful working hours.

How to arrange a low radial carnation vase

Step 1: We start to soak the flower arrangement sponge in water for 30 - 1 hour. Note that the soaking time is more or less depending on the type of flower arrangement foam separately.

Note, do not drop the sponge submerged in water, leaving it for too long will cause the sponge to fall apart. The best tip is to put the sponge in a box/bowl, fill it with water 1/3 - 1/2 of the sponge, and then let it absorb the water slowly. This method helps to absorb the water evenly and this is also a way to help arrange carnations for a long time. To test the softness of the sponge, gently press your finger on the foam surface to check, if it forms and feels the sponge melts slightly.

Step 2: Finish preparing the carnation foam, you trim the foam so that it fits the mouth of the vase, forming half a sphere at the top. Place the styrofoam in the vase so that the spherical part of the foam protrudes from the mouth of the vase for easy handling of flower arrangements. Secure with clear tape to prevent the foam from loosening or falling out of the jar when moving. Carnation vase lights up your small corner room

Step 3: Estimate the height of the flower to customize it to fit in the vase. Choose a carnation stem with the largest flower size for shaping. Then you stick that cotton in the center position of the foam.

Step 4: Plug the carnations in a symmetrical shape to form a circle around, radiating out.

Step 5: Use weasel tail leaves or Trac Bach Diep that can be purchased at fresh flower shops to plug in the remaining gaps to fill in the blanks. With that, your carnation vase is done. This way of arranging carnations is often used by people during Tet, so you should remember to decorate the living room during the upcoming Tet holiday.

Arrange Purple Salem Flowers

The meaning of purple Salem flowers

Because of their long-lasting properties, salem flowers are often chosen to convey messages and symbols for permanence, sustainability or something forever. Besides, the salem flower also symbolizes the good humility of people.

Giving each other a bouquet of salem flowers is a great idea to express feelings of longing and a message of a strong and intense love that will last forever. In addition, salem flowers also bring a message of joy and peace when always bringing a sense of peace.

It is also because of the good meanings that salem flowers bring, that this flower is often chosen as a congratulatory flower, as a gift and as a decoration in the house.

You can use it to decorate the living room, dining room, office or display it on a flower stand, window. To breathe fresh life into the space.

To arrange a beautiful flower basket, harmoniously coordinate many different flowers. You need to prepare the following materials: Flowers for the arrangement: yellow chrysanthemums, purple chrysanthemums, orange carnations, salem flowers, purple cassava flowers, silver branches... A clear rattan basket, a water vase round crystal.

A tissue blotting or nylon flower wrapping paper. Styrofoam flower arrangements and tools to cut flower branches.

Instructions on how to arrange purple salem flowers

After preparing all the materials and tools, we proceed to arrange flowers according to the following steps:

Step 1: First, use scissors to cut the flower arrangement foam into the glass vase, notice that the foam surface will be higher than the mouth of the vase and higher than the height of the iron basket. Soak the sponge evenly in water before performing flower arrangements.

Next, you cut the raw fabric into a rectangular sheet and put it in the basket and put the glass jar in the middle. Use scissors to cut the branches vertically and perpendicularly to the foam surface in the middle of the vase.

You cut and plug 2 branches of orange carnations close to the foam surface in two opposite directions, you direct the flower outward. You cut and plug 2 branches of purple chrysanthemums close to the foam surface, in opposite directions, between 2 branches of orange carnations.

Step 2: Next, you cut and plug the branches of yellow chrysanthemums

alternately, with a height lower than the flower branch and higher than the cut flower branch to create an arch. Intersperse the salem branches and silver leaf branches between the chrysanthemum branches. Check the vase one more time, if there is an empty space, you can add chrysanthemums to cover the foam surface.

A handmade flower basket with full colors: blue salem, yellow chrysanthemum, orange carnation, purple sage flower together with green color of leaves blend harmoniously and well. The iron basket with terracotta cloth has brought a rustic but no less delicate feature to this flower basket.

Arrange Beautiful Rum Flower

Instructions on how to arrange beautiful Rum flowers

Ingredient:

- Safflower: 3 white flowers, 2 yellow green flowers, 3 yellow flowers. You can spray paint white safflower flowers instead of buying flowers.
- Orange cypress flowers: 7 to 10 flowers. If you only buy purple cypress flowers, you should choose the main flower not in blue-yellow-white tones but purple-pink-white, so it will be more harmonious.
- A few branches and leaves of different sizes to plug in the color background
- 5 large jewelry stones and pointed buds like flower buds (same color as cypress flowers) are inserted into the ends of small bamboo skewers, so choose two or 3 dark tones close to each other.
- Small flower pots (such as terracotta pots), flower arrangement foam and large ribbons for bowing

Perform:

Step 1:

To follow this glitter trinket flower arrangement, you need to create a natural blue background for the striking flowers and stones.

You cut the foam to fit into the pot of the small flower arrangement, absorb enough water for the foam, plug the large leaves around the edge of the pot, the green leaf face facing out.

Step 2:

You cut short the safflower and plug 3 white flowers into a right corner of the pot, plug 3 yellow flowers into the left corner of the pot, plug 2 blue and white flowers into the intersection between the two colors white and yellow but direct the flowers to the front. Then plug small branches and leaves around to cover the flower stalks and spongy surface.

Step 3:

You arrange the cypress flowers to extend out the pot a little for a natural look. It is the center of the front half of the flower pot that focuses the eyes of the flower watcher the most, you plug the large stones and stretch out along the daisies.

If you don't have jewelry stones, you can use plastic beads with a similar shape.

Step 4:

Finally, you use the body of the leftover rum flower to bend it into two round straps plugged into the two ends of the flower pot mouth, to cross the two straps for more tone.

Let's tie a bow to make your small flower pot more charming! The flower pot looks both natural and boldly stylized, the stone beads harmonize with the flowers, making them look like the incarnation of cypress daisies, and the colors of the three-color safflower are vivid.

Arrange Bell Flowers

Legend of the Bellflower

Legend has it that the goddess of love and beauty, Venus, had a magic mirror. This mirror makes anyone who looks at himself become a very beautiful person. One day, the magic mirror was unfortunately lost. Then a shepherd boy found a magic mirror. Day by day, he gradually began to enjoy looking at himself in the mirror. So he decided to keep guongw to himself.

When she heard that the mirror had fallen into the shepherd's hands, Venus immediately sent Cupid to Earth to retrieve the mirror. But the shepherd did not want to return the mirror. So Cupid used his arrow to shoot the shepherd. At that moment, the magic mirror was thrown from the shepherd's hand and broke. From that broken mirror gradually appeared bellflowers of different colors.

What are the meanings of the Bellflower tree?
Bellflower is a unique and brilliant flower, making those who look at it fall in love with it. The meaning of the Bell flower is to express gratitude, sincerity and endless gratitude. Bellflower also symbolizes a new beginning, a new journey and enthusiasm and luck at work. Sometimes it even shows longevity, nothing can be changed. In addition, the bell flower also shows the shyness and shyness of a girl in the green spring.

How to arrange Bell flowers

Step 1: It is necessary to cut the root diagonally. Therefore, it is easier to use stars or sharp scissors. Dried bellflowers should not be cut to prevent air from entering. Then, pick up all the leaves near the base, the leaves that are below the surface of the vase.

Step 2: Use newspaper or nylon to wrap flowers. It has tiny holes to let the steam out and wrap the bouquet. To keep the flowers fresh for a long time, it is necessary to soak the flowers in warm water and add a flower conditioner. Each such batch is about 3-5 times depending on conditions and time.

Step 3: Need to rely on flower buds to watch the rest time from 1 to 2 days. Then bring the official cotton plug into the vase. To be able to display flowers for a long time, you must change the water once a day, cut the root and wash the vase. Each time like that, there are 3/6 times replaced with warm water.

Step 4: If we see that the Bellflower has wilted, we need to drop the flower branch into a large pot. This will help the flower stems get enough water and fresh again.

Step 5: Bellflowers can be planted for a long time, the average time is from 7 to 10 days. So you can unleash your creativity with your flower vases to bring out the most unique flower vases.

Wild Bird Flower

Wild bird flower arrangement

Like its name, the bird of paradise flower has very unique contours. Like the image of a mythical bird heading to heaven.

The color of the flower is in natural harmony between the color of the flower and the color of the leaves.

Plug way:

2 celestial birds are racing on one side

The other 1 flower is plugged in the opposite direction like a bird looking forward to follow the flock.

It will be very suitable if you arrange bird's eye flowers with large lobed leaves. The leaf style is like a symbol of the wild Hawaiian land.

Add 2 large flowers of the same color to the side of the vase. I imagine like a color connection between the earth and the sky that the celestial bird is aiming for.

5 ways to arrange flowers Heavenly birds bring soul to beautiful vases

This type of flower arrangement with lines rising like the intense vitality of wild plants. At the same time, like a flock of birds in the sky towards the depths of nature.

Heather Flower Arrangement

Materials:

- Flowers to arrange:
- 1 big bunch purple
- 5 fern leaves
- Glass flower vase
- 1 piece of white ribbon
- Scissors cut flower branches

2. Make a heather flower arrangement:

Step 1: Pour water into the flowerpot to keep the flowers fresh longer.

Step 2: Strip off all the leaves, arrange the tops of the heather branches on top of each other and then bunch them into a big round heather bunch. Then, cut off the base and use tape to secure the bouquet and put it in the vase. After plugging, you remember to adjust so that the flower branches spread evenly in all directions to make the vase look more beautiful.

Step 3: Finally, you can add your flowerpot with some ferns around the mouth of the jar. In addition, attaching a white bow at the mouth of the jar is also a good idea that can partially cover the flower branches and the mouth of the jar, while also enhancing the elegance and grace of your finished product.

Arrange Beautiful Apricot Flowers

What is apricot blossom?

Snow apricot flowers (also known as snow white flowers apricot, code Thien Huong, or flowers thousands of stars...).

Snowflakes in the forest have small, thin branches, tiny green leaves, and white flowers like snowflakes on a wooden trunk. Smell carefully to see the light aroma from the petals and woody stems.

2. The origin of apricot blossom

Snow apricot flowers originate from China. Flowers usually bloom in late winter and early spring. Flowers are white, tiny, very pretty. This flower has a light, pleasant fragrance. Therefore, besides the beauty, the fragrance is also the attraction of apricot snow.

Each flower spike has a length between 1.2m and 1.5m. Flowers have 5 petals, white color, tiny, very pretty. Flowers and leaves grow along the branches in dense density. Therefore, although the flowers and leaves are small in size, the whole flower branch is very luxuriant and attractive.

Snow apricot flowers, which originate from China and bloom in early spring, have an ethereal and elegant beauty with small white flowers. Is a type of imported flower that is quite popular in recent times. Flowers have fragile and pure beauty, so they won the hearts of many people. Let's study with Nguyet Hy flower palace through some of the main features as well as the meaning of apricot flowers.

3. How to choose to buy apricot blossom

Should choose branches that have both flowers and buds for a longer playing time.

Priority is given to scenes where flowers and leaves are close together. Choose fresh flowers that are not wilted or crushed because once they are shared, other branches may also be affected.

In a vase, there should be both straight and curved branches to create the most natural harmony.

4. How to choose a beautiful apricot blossom vase

Like other flowers, apricot flowers can be arranged in many different styles. However, choosing a suitable vase is not easy because the apricot tree branch is quite long.

With the elegance of this flower, people often choose tall ceramic vases. The tall and large vase is suitable for large living rooms, on the contrary, if your living room is not too large, you should choose a tall slim vase and flower arrangements that do not need to be too wide.

5. How to arrange beautiful apricot flowers

You can refer to How to arrange apricot flowers specifically as follows:

Step 1: Snow apricot flowers are woody flowers that are difficult to absorb water. Therefore, before planting, you should cut the flower base diagonally to about 45 degrees, and at the same time, split the root so that the flower can absorb water more easily.

Step 2: You should proceed to burn the flower stem on a gas stove or wood stove to limit the growth of bacteria that cause rotten branches.

Step 3: To make the flowers last longer, put water in the flower vase and then put some flower balm or vitamin B1 tablets or crush aspirin and drop it into the vase.

Step 4: You plug the apricot blossom branches in turn into the vase. It is advisable to intertwine the straight and curved branches so that the overall vase has the most softness and harmony.

Step 5: Finally, after the plug is complete, place the vase in a cool, well-lit location, away from heat sources. You should change the water for flowers once every 2 days, and at the same time spray mist on the flower branches to keep the flowers fresh longer.

Arrange Lily

Prepare:

- 1 tall ceramic vase
- 1 piece of foam
- 20 ornamental coconut leaves
- 60 lily branches
- Spotted bamboo leaves
- Tools: Scissors, tape

Doing:

The first step: You fix the sponge and the mouth of the bottle tightly.

Step 2: Cut the edge of the coconut leaf in a pyramid shape. Insert the highest first card into the edge of the sponge, the next two cards are symmetrically inserted and about 5cm lower than the main leaf.

Step 3: You choose 8 straight lily branches plugged in the middle, the highest flower is close to the central coconut leaf, the remaining branches are lower, the height is 2/3 of the coconut leaf.

Step 4: You stick other lily branches staggered, lower down to the bottom of the sponge, the lily branches point out, 2/3 up and the lowest floor towards the bottom to cover the sponge.

Step 5: Then, insert spotted bamboo leaves between the gaps of the lily to cover the sponge.

Step 6: Use the remaining coconut leaves around the vase in a conical shape.

Arrange Violets

Be prepared:

- 3 bunches of purple violets (cut into small stems)
- 1 piece of foam, 1 wide-mouthed white flower vase.

Prepare violets for planting

The process of arranging a beautiful and unique violet flower vase:
When buying flowers, cut off leaves and flower branches, soak the sponge in water to slowly suck it up. When you see that the foam does not absorb water anymore, take it out, put the sponge in the bottle and pour water to the mouth of the bottle, then use white tape to fix the sponge to the bottle.

First, arrange the violets first. Sisters cut 10 violet branches with a height of 45-50cm and put them in the middle of the vase, the height of the next violet layer is 5-10cm higher than the previous one, creating a soft round shape.
First, plug the big flowers with clear colors, showing the beauty in the 4 corners of the vase, 4 smaller flowers will be alternately plugged into the 4 corners we just plugged earlier. Plug so that the cotton is high, the cotton is low, the cotton on the lower cotton has a minimum distance of 2cm.

The remaining small flowers, we put the last one below to create a softness and balance between the violet flowers above.

The vase of violets makes the home space more beautiful

Tips to help beautiful and long-lasting violet vases:

The tips in how to arrange beautiful violets is that you should prune all the leaves at the flower stalk that is submerged in water. Leaves of flowers are the main cause of the water quickly stink. The upper flower branch only needs to be trimmed off a part of the leaves so that the vase has a more elegant and graceful appearance.

Besides flower arranging water, you can add a little dishwashing liquid to prevent the growth of bacteria, helping flowers stay fresh for 2-3 times longer. Since violets absorb a lot of water, it needs to be added daily. Just a little lack of water and delicate violets will wilt instantly.

The next thing is to choose a white porcelain vase, with a certain softness and grace, and arrange the bouquets inside the vase in a way that you feel like. After plugging, you should add a few flower branches to create a natural beauty for the vase.

The space is full of life when the vase of violets is next to the window

A fact proves that, your living space will be beautiful, different, and impressive thanks to these beautiful purple heart flower bouquets. Not only roses, chrysanthemums can beautify the space. Any flower that you like, any arrangement you feel "just right" can help make the space more beautiful and impressive.

Arrange Iris Flower

Ingredient

- Irises, conifers
- Flower Cages (you can buy them at some major florists)
- Lichen, porcelain podium, scissors..

Making

1. After buying flowers and tools, you choose a few conifers to separate and then cut into pieces of conifers with the size of 50, 40, 32cm.

First, cut each piece of conifer tree with the size of 50, 40, 32cm

2. Iris when buying should choose fresh flowers, do not bloom too big, you just need to buy budding buds, after a few days it will bloom. Cut the iris stem into lengths of 17.5.12.5,7.5cm diameter.

Cut the iris stem into 17.5.12.5,7.5cm . segments

3. Start arranging irises! First you put the plug cage on the porcelain platform. Then plug the cypress into the cage in order from left to right.

Plug the cypress into the cage, then arrange the interlaced blue irises

4. Blue irises will be planted in ascending order from outside to inside.

The arrangement of blue iris flowers in turn from the outside to the inside in ascending order is to complete the arrangement of blue iris flowers.

The arrangement of blue iris flowers in turn from the outside to the inside in ascending order is to complete the arrangement of blue iris flowers.
Finished product

Add lichens around the porcelain podium and you're done. The gentle green iris flowers combined with green leaves and grass bring freshness and vitality to the space.

With Japanese flower arrangement style, it will be quite suitable if your home has a modest area or the rooms have a simple interior style. On the contrary, if your home has a more sophisticated and formal style, consider replacing the Japanese-style flower clusters with large and luxurious vases of lilies.

Arrange Wolf Muzzle Flower

The wolf snout flower has the scientific name Antirrhinum majus L, belongs to the wolf muzzle family (Scrophulariaceae). The flower is also known as the flower of the dog's muzzle, the goat's edge, the dragon's snout, the needle fish... The wolf's snout belongs to a tall herbaceous plant that lives every year.

The inflorescence at the end of the stem bears many large flowers that are regularly spaced and bloom from bottom to top. The flower has corolla divided into 2 lips, the two sides are squeezed together, looking like the jaws of an animal when expanded. Flowers are diverse in types and have many different colors.

The wolf muzzle flower symbolizes a bright future. You can send flowers on the occasion of housewarming, grand opening or birthday celebration. And how to arrange wolf muzzle flowers is also very simple and easy to do, please refer to the article below!

1. Raw materials:

Flowers to arrange:
- 3 branches of wolf muzzle flower
- 2 fern leaves
- Tall glass bottles (such as wine bottles)
- Scissors cut flower branches

How to arrange beautiful and simple wolf muzzle flower

2. How to do it:

Step 1: Put water in 2/3 of the bottle. You can add a few crushed aspirin tablets to the flower arrangement to keep the flowers fresh longer.

Step 2: Insert the wolf muzzle flower into the bottle with different heights. You should test the length of the flower before cutting so that the flower is not too low. Remove all the leaves at the base and stem because when the leaves get wet, it will quickly make the flowers wilt and quickly stink.

Step 3: Stick the fern leaf close to the mouth of the bottle, leaning in one direction.

With a beautiful and simple wolf muzzle flower arrangement, you can decorate this small vase on the dining table, study table, dressing table or window frame as you like. Also, placing it next to a few similarly pretty vases for a more lively look is also a great idea.

Arrange Ranunculus Flowers

Prepare

- 1 bunch of ranunculus flowers, pay attention to choose both large and small flowers and buds, do not choose evenly large flowers.
- 1 bunch of small branches and leaves like mulberry leaves, apple leaves, bamboo shoots...
- 1 bunch of pretty small flowers like heather, mimoza, star flower, baby flower...
- 1 bunch of grass flowers in the form of white crested flowers or small, long flowers like willows, auspicious flowers, kodemari flowers...
- Low square vase.
- Flower arrangement.

Doing

Step 1: Before starting to arrange flowers, you must cut the foam to fit the vase and then soak the sponge in a pot full of water. When the foam is full of water, take it out, put it in the vase, and cut the square corners of the foam to increase the flower arrangement area.

Step 2: Then, you plug a large leaf branch on the left corner of the sponge and a smaller branch at the bottom right corner of the sponge, so that the 2 branches form a diagonal line. Next, you use shorter branches to spread evenly around and close to the mouth of the vase.

Step 3: Plug the extra flower branches around so that the flowers spread evenly on the mouth of the vase. However, because you arrange the flowers according to the first two branches, the flower shape will not be round, but will form a diagonal oval created by those two branches.

Step 4: Arrange ranunculus flowers alternately and spread evenly according to the shape of the auxiliary flowers, pay attention to the large flowers in the middle of the vase, the smaller flowers will gradually spread to the sides and the flower buds will be attached to the tops of the long leaves. the outermost.

Step 5: Finally, you arrange the tall grass flowers alternately around the mouth of the vase so that these flower branches do not cover the flowers in the middle.

Arrange Poppy lowers

Poppy flowers planted in the flower garden make you feel like you are seeing a bunch of beautiful girls dancing, with all sorts of poses. The poppy plant attracts the eye with a variety of colors such as yellow, red, pink, and white

When buying, people cut the root and soak it in water for a few hours, please arrange it because any flower from the time of cutting, shipping and reaching the consumer is already weak.

After 2-6 hours, start arranging flowers in the vase.

Step 1: The most important thing is to choose a flower vase (the same color as any flower branch is easy to match). 2 bunches of Poppy to fit the mouth of the bottle about 8-9cm

Step 2: When the old flower buds are slightly open, gently peel them off with your hands to make the flowers bloom easily

Step 3:

Determine the right side so that the beautiful face shows the direction of the plug.

Stick the bent branch first

The 3 flowers next to each other have different blooms and are not on the same plane.

Multiple Flower Holding

Prepare materials:

- Rose
- hydrangeas
- Pink lilies
- Wall orchids
- A few sprigs of bird's nest
- A few branches of orchids are happy
- Some branches of swallow wings
- Leaf fern
- Bamboo leaves

Arrange a beautiful 2-tier flower basket:

Step 1: First, you cut the flower stem diagonally to the right size, the flowers arranged on the outside edge are longer than the flower branches inside.

Step 2: Plug the fern and bamboo branches into the flower arrangement foam at the edge to determine the form of the flower basket.

Then arrange roses, hydrangeas, pink lilies and wall orchids accordingly. As many flowers as you like, in accordance with the size of the flower basket you want. As for hydrangeas, you should choose only 3 flowers, large flowers will overwhelm other flowers if you plug too many flowers.

Step 3: Next, you plug the extra flower branches up, fill the gaps on the flower basket so that it is reasonable and eye-catching. Should be evenly distributed and harmonious colors to increase the aesthetics of the 2-tier flower basket.

Step 4: After completing the above steps, you have a complete 2-tier basket.

This is a guide on how to arrange the opening flower basket, if you want to arrange a funeral flower basket, you can choose condolence flowers with other colors. The 2-tier funeral flower arrangement is similar to the above, it's easy to do, isn't it!

You can buy extra water called "flower food" to add nutrients, help flowers stay fresh longer. Add warm water above 22 degrees Celsius to the foam, place the 2-tier flower basket in a cool place, avoid direct sunlight.

Arrangement Mix
Peonies double Lilies

Prepare materials

- Rose
- hydrangeas
- Pink lilies
- Wall orchids
- A few sprigs of bird's nest
- A few branches of orchids are happy
- Some branches of swallow wings
- Leaf fern
- Bamboo leaves

Arrange a beautiful 2-tier flower basket:

Step 1: First, you cut the flower stem diagonally to the right size, the flowers arranged on the outside edge are longer than the flower branches inside.

Step 2: Plug the fern and bamboo branches into the flower arrangement foam at the edge to determine the form of the flower basket.

Then arrange roses, hydrangeas, pink lilies and wall orchids accordingly. As many flowers as you like, in accordance with the size of the flower basket you want. As for hydrangeas, you should choose only 3 flowers, large flowers will overwhelm other flowers if you plug too many flowers.

Step 3: Next, you plug the extra flower branches up, fill the gaps on the flower basket so that it is reasonable and eye-catching. Should be evenly distributed and harmonious colors to increase the aesthetics of the 2-tier flower basket.

Step 4: After completing the above steps, you have a complete 2-tier basket. This is a guide on how to arrange the opening flower basket, if you want to arrange a funeral flower basket, you can choose condolence flowers with other colors. The 2-tier funeral flower arrangement is similar to the above, it's easy to do, isn't it!

You can buy extra water called "flower food" to add nutrients, help flowers stay fresh longer. Add warm water above 22 degrees Celsius to the foam, place the 2-tier flower basket in a cool place, avoid direct sunlight.

Japanese Style Gerbera Arrangement

Prepare:

- 5 red gerbera flowers and its leaves
- 2 small bonsai pots, small leaves like bonsai
- Some branches live forever
- 5 small dandelion leaves or ornamental leaves
- 1 horizontal rectangular flower arrangement tray, transparent glass material
- Small pebbles of the same color (enough to fill half a glass tray): you can buy it at an aquarium or home decor store.
- Styrofoam flower arrangement
- Scissors, knife, water

Making:

1. In this gerbera arrangement, the flower looks very natural like it's grown from a pot, but you actually have to stick it in the flower arrangements. Styrofoam cut into 5 bars 2cm wide and about 5cm long, soaked in water.

Color gravel washed, filled 1/3 of the glass tray.

2. Two mini bonsai clumps are separated from the pot, leaving the soil monolithic. You push the gravel to the side to put two clusters of plants on the ends of the tray, then again put the gravel around the base of the tree, placing the tree so that its soil surface is level with the mouth of the tray.

3. Each dong leaf is rolled up, the heart of the leaf roll is 2cm wide enough to stuff the flower arrangement foam in the middle. Use a pin or sharp toothpick to pin the leaves to stabilize the shape.

Refurbish bowls for flower arrangements
Instructions on how to arrange beautiful flowers for a fresher summer
A unique way to arrange chrysanthemums for a splendid party
Arrange 5 leaf rolls vertically in the middle of the glass tray, staggered high and low before and after for a beautiful look. Drop more gravel around the leaf rolls to keep them steady

4. Cut gerbera 12cm - 15cm long and stick it between the leaf rolls that you have inserted the flower arrangement foam inside. Fill the tray with gravel and fill it with water 2/3 of the way.

You stick a few coin leaves spread evenly around the mouth of the tray for nature, next to each leaf is a segment of the stem of a living tree so that later it will sprout natural sprouts to replace the coin leaves. This gerbera arrangement does not require you to pose a lot of flowers, just arrange the flowers in a natural direction like when it grows in the garden.

The crimson gerbera flowers, prominent in the rolled leaves, create a harmony with the image of fresh sushi rolled in seaweed leaves on the dining table. A very Japanese flower arrangement!

You can replace gerbera with other flowers depending on the color of the interior around your flower tray. As long as you keep the natural style like a gerbera in this gerbera arrangement: simple, elegant, harmonize colors and lines between leaves and flowers, between flower trays and furniture, etc.

lower Arrangement Shape Of A Birthday Cake

Prepare:

- Carnations or chrysanthemums with many small petals: two different colors, about 20 flowers each color, you cut off the flower stalks, leaving only about 2cm.
- Chrysanthemums have wide petals and clear wing lines to cover the top: about 10 flowers
- Styrofoam flower arrangement: cut Styrofoam in half to get 1 square block and then cut and cut the corners evenly to gradually form a round foam block, drop the Styrofoam into a flooded pot to let it absorb water gradually.
- A plate of birthday cakes
- Scissors, if you like, you can have more decorative accessories such as ribbons, large beads, birthday candles, etc.
-

Making:

1. This flower arrangement is like a birthday cake, so you need a birthday cake-type plate to create a natural, lifelike feel. Put the sponge on the plate of the birthday cake, arrange the yellow carnations close to the bottom of the sponge, plug a circle around the sponge to form the first cake layer.

2. Next, you arrange the pink carnations into a circle following the first yellow wreath. The stalks of the two garlands are arranged close together, about 1cm to 2cm apart (depending on how big or small your flower is). You may have to press down on the yellow petals a bit during the pink flower arrangement, so the petals will spring back into place and create a more snug feel. Similarly, you add a second pink wreath (or more rings) to seal the foam wall. The top garland may have to be slanted down if the styrofoam is tight.

3. At the top of the "flower cake", you fill the circle with chrysanthemums and or flowers with clear lines. The purpose of using flowers other than this wing style is to make the cake surface more prominent, clearly see the flowers. The wall of the cake is just to create the color array, so carnations or small chrysanthemums are very suitable.

4. You use the stamens (remove the petals) to decorate around the cake, can be replaced with small balls skewered in toothpicks, or ribbons and many other accessories of your choice. Put the flower cake in the cake box as a birthday gift, the gift recipient will be very surprised when opening it!

The basic principle of the birthday cake flower arrangement is to create the background color of the cake, decorate it vividly and the most beautiful flowers are displayed on the cake. The method is simple, but the color variation on the flower cake is very diverse.

Flower Arrangement attan Basket

You need to prepare:

- Light green hydrangea: 3 branches
- Blue carnation
- White orchid: 5 branches
- White gerbera: 1 bunch (can be replaced with large white chrysanthemums)
- White pansy
- Small branches and leaves (can be used with baby flowers interspersed on flower baskets)
- Rattan flower basket, nylon bag, small zinc thread
- Styrofoam flower arrangement, scissors to cut flower branches

How to arrange flowers as follows:

Step 1:

First, you put the plastic bag in the rattan basket, gently press the bag inside the nylon bag so that it sticks to the inside of the basket, cut off the excess bag above the rim of the basket and tie it up with zinc wire. . The nylon bag keeps the sponge moist without damaging the basket.

Step 2:

Cut a large rectangular white nylon sheet and place it in the basket. Next, cut a large foam sheet and place it on a white nylon sheet in a basket. Use a zinc wire to tie two on the side of the handle with two branches to keep it fixed so that the foam sheet does not fall off, and the nylon bags are spread out to the sides. Remember to soak the foam sheet in water first.

White Roses And Purple Stars

Roses for plugging are 15-23 branches of white-blue roses, white-pink roses, red roses or yellow roses. You should choose to buy Dalat roses with large flowers, the flowerpot will look more beautiful.

If the rose has a flower that is too small, it will fit in the vase and be out of balance. You can add a bunch of purple stars in this beautiful and cute rose arrangement.

- Glass vase with legs
- Crystal beads (glass earth) (if any)
- Scissors cut flower branches really sharp

Materials for the arrangement of white roses and purple stars

2. How to arrange white roses and star flowers How to arrange beautiful roses
Step 1: If you don't have glass beads, you can simply fill 2/3 of the vase with water. If you have crystals, the vase will look more shimmery. You need to soak the glass beads in water for the seeds to expand (about 6-8 hours). After soaking, you can discard the excess water and rinse again to be able to use.

Step 2: Arrange the purple star flowers evenly with a length equal to 2 times the height of the flowerpot and then cut off the base. Then, put purple star flowers in the vase, adjust so that the flowers spread evenly in all directions. For some of you who like simplicity, this purple star flower vase is already considered a finished product.

Step 3: You plug the white rose branches into alternating between the purple star flowers in a circular shape.

Depending on your personal preferences, you can add or subtract the number of purple star flowers. This arrangement of roses will have 2 different results: the vase of roses with few purple star flowers looks more luxurious and elegant; and the vase of roses interspersed with many purple stars will have a more natural, wild direction.

Arrange Beautiful And Tender Roses With Carnations And Lilies

Materials for how to arrange beautiful roses

- With the soft pink color of pinkish-pink roses, you can mix it with the pure white and fresh pink of carnations and lilies will be a great choice for a good day.
-
- Flowers for arrangement: 3 branches of pink lilies; 10 branches of pink roses; 7 branches of white carnations
- Tall glass jar
- Scissors cut flower branches

Ingredients for a beautiful rose arrangement

Step 1: Pour water into the flowerpot to keep the flowers fresh for a long time. Use sticky tape to create a checkered pattern on the top of the vase to keep the flowers steady and evenly distributed in the jar.

Step 2: Cut the flower stem and place the pink lilies in the vase first, adjusting the flowers to spread evenly in all directions.

Step 3: Insert carnations and roses in between the lilies, adjusting so that the flowers spread evenly in all directions.

With this beautiful arrangement of roses combined with lilies and carnations, you can put this flowerpot on the ancestral table, in the living room or kitchen to breathe new life into your home space. it takes too much time.

White Baby Hand Held Wedding Bouquet

Prepare flowers and tools

- 1-2 bouquets of white baby flowers
- Small ropes specialized for bouquets
- Small Ribbons
- Scissors

Step 1: Carefully select each white baby branch, cut off the wilted flower branches.

Step 2: Arrange the short flower spikes on the inside of the bouquet. The flower spikes are longer on the outside of the bouquet. Continue doing this until you feel comfortable, then stop.

Note: Arrange the flower stems so that they form an even radial bouquet.

Step 3: Use ribbon to wrap around the handle of the bouquet.

Step 4: Use scissors to cut off the longer flower stems at the handle of the bouquet so that the flower branches are equal.

Step 5: Continue to wrap the handle of the bouquet with rope to decorate the bouquet.

Remember to leave a small piece at the handle of the bouquet so that you can dip it in the jar. This will help keep the bouquet fresh for longer.

Not only carrying auspicious meanings, the wedding bouquet made from white baby flowers can be easily combined with all different styles of wedding dresses.

Hold Bouquet Of Roses In The Bride's Hand

Prepare:

25 beautiful imported roses. Should choose the same flowers, should not bloom too big, petals are not crushed, branches are straight, flower colors match the wedding dress, or your preferences.

- 1 single coil in metallic color of your choice
- 1 Flower cutting scissors
- 2 small pins
- 1 bottle of colorless hairspray
- A little is acacia, moldy leaves, grass leaves, baby flowers, etc. (if you don't have it, it's okay, you can also use rose leaves)
- Tools along the leaves, along the spines (you can not have them)
- 1 Small roll of adhesive tape

How to hold a beautiful bouquet of roses in the bride's hand

Step 1: Prepare roses: After buying roses, cut off the thorns and leaves, with a tool along the leaves, if you don't have them, you can use scissors to cut and remove the thorns, pay attention to not be pricked by the thorns. Place the cut rose in a jar of water and let it sit for 3 to 4 hours for the flowers to soak in the water.

Step 2: Next, you choose the most beautiful rose as the center and arrange 3 other flowers around it

Step 3: Use adhesive tape to fix the 4 flowers just made. It is recommended to wrap adhesive tape about 10 cm from the calyx

Step 4: Add 3 other flowers and fix them with adhesive tape as in step 3. Step add flowers like that until all the roses are prepared. Note that when adding flowers, you need to align so that the round bouquet is evenly balanced, use adhesive tape to fix each time adding flowers to keep the shape of the bouquet firmly.

Step 5: The tape pants are tight and round so that the tape is in the palm of your hand

Step 6: Check that the bouquet is round and firm when holding, if not, fix it

How to hold a beautiful bouquet of roses in the bride's hand
How to hold a beautiful bouquet of roses in the bride's hand

Step 7: Use here only the prepared metallic tape to cover the adhesive tape in turn, we wrap it from top to bottom and vice versa from bottom to top to make sure.

Step 8: After wrapping the tape in turn to cover the adhesive tape, we cut off the excess tape

Step 9: Use the tape to fix the end of the tape so that it does not slip, stick the pins directly into the flower branches in the direction from top to bottom

Step 10: Add 1 more recorder to hold the ribbon

Step 11: Cut off the excess flower stalk from 2 to 3cm . away

Step 12: Use colorless hairspray to gently spray on the bouquet to keep the flowers fresh for a longer time

Baby Flower Crown

You need to prepare the following ingredients:

- Baby flower
- Zinc wire
- Flower arrangement tape
- Zinc cutting pliers
- Decorative ribbons
- Color spray paint

Step 1: Measure and shape

Use a wire wrapped lightly around the head to estimate the bride's head circumference. Then use pliers to cut the excess zinc and find the middle of that piece of zinc. Fold the zinc in half and secure the shape by twisting together. So your wreath has a basic shape already. To make the wreath secure, put your index finger in the double of the zinc ring and then gently bend it to create a hook, hook it to the connector.

Step 2: Use duct tape

Choose green tape to give the wreath some color. Wrap the tape around the wire continuously and maybe add some colorful tape to make the wreath more pretty. Note that you should choose the color of the tape to match the color of the wedding decoration.

Step 3: Prune flower branches

This is the step to take before attaching flowers to the wedding ring. You need to prune the flower branches so that the length of the flower branches is the same. Should use iron pliers to cut instead of scissors, so the branch will not be crushed or broken. Before you attach the flowers to the wedding ring, you should prune the branches to the same length

Step 4: Attach flowers to the ring

This is a step that requires you to be very careful and meticulous. You can decide to put the flowers horizontally or vertically in the most beautiful way. After placing the flowers, use tape to wrap around the flower branches to fix the position of the flowers. Note, arrange flower branches in the same direction to make it easier to attach flowers.

Salem Flower Headband

Materials needed to prepare include

White salem flowers
Thin, malleable wire
Green tape
Zinc cutting pliers
Decorative ribbons

Step 1: Just like the baby wreath, you need to wrap the zinc around your head to determine the circumference of your wreath. Continue to cut a piece of zinc 3 times its length and fold it three times, twisting the zinc will form a fixed frame of the garland.

Step 2: You wrap the zinc ring by wrapping a lot of green tape around it. Note that wrapping as many loops as possible in a row is better because it will make the ring more compact and softer. Do not wrap too thick because it both makes the bride's head heavy and makes it difficult to attach flowers.

Step 3: Prune the salem lilies before planting

The reasonable length for salem flower branches to make wreaths is from 5cm - 7cm. You should prune flower stems to this length. Note that the original part should be left blank, leaving a little extra to make it easier to stick together.

Step 4: Insert the salem flowers into the zinc ring

Place each salem flower stem in a clockwise direction, use tape to stick the base of the flower stem with a zinc ring. Note: When wrapping, please tighten it tightly so that the flowers do not become loose or accidentally fall off during the wedding ceremony.

Wedding Flowers Head With Fresh Flowers

Colorful fresh flowers will make the wreath interesting and attractive.

Materials to prepare:

Fresh flowers
Thin steel wire or copper wire for easy crimping
Pliers and scissors
Ribbons
Tape

Step 1: Cut 10 thin pieces of steel into 10cm lengths and then round them together. Wrap the tape tightly around the zinc frames so they don't come apart.

Step 2: Cut the roots, flower stems, leaving only a 5cm length of flower stalks. For flower branches with many branches, they should be divided into small branches.

Step 3: Start using blue tape to wrap the flowers in the zinc frame, carefully wrapping from the flower body. You should wrap flowers alternating colors to create a variety and eye-catching. Note that you should arrange so that the flower stem protrudes from the bottom. This way you can easily wrap other flower spikes.

For fresh wreaths, you should add more emphasis by adding large flowers. Cut the flower as close to the base as you can and then thread the flower into the wire. Continue to attach to the wreath, bend the wire end a bit so that the wire hooks into the ring frame!

Step 4: To decorate the wreath more eye-catching, tie the fabric ribbon to the ends of the wreath. Should choose white, light yellow, light pink ribbons very suitable for the wedding atmosphere.

Arrange Roses In Tall Vases

Prepare flowers

- Long roses: 10-15 branches
- Assorted flowers and leaves for decoration
- Tall jars (glass or porcelain jars optional)
- Scissors or sharp knife
- Bleach/mouthwash or lemon juice
- Steps to put roses in tall vases

To have a fresh and beautiful flower vase, you must first wash the vase with dishwashing liquid, then dry it and prepare the flower arrangement.

Step 1: You should not use cold water, but use flower arrangement from 35-40 degrees Celsius. Mix a little bleach, mouthwash or lemon juice into the water for the purpose of keeping the flowers fresh longer. after plugging.

Step 2: Gently clean the rose branches with water to remove all soil, sand and dust still clinging to the branches. Use scissors to cut off the entire flower leaf at the end of the flower stem.

Step 3: After the flowers have been cleaned, use a sharp knife or scissors to cut the beveled branches of the rose at a 45-degree angle, paying attention to cut the flower branches of different lengths to easily shape the vase.

Step 4: Insert the longest cut rose stems into the middle of the vase. In turn, arrange shorter flower stems around to form a sphere for the flowerpot.

Step 5: Plug in the extra flowers alternating between the roses to create accents. You can add extra leaves or choose additional flowers such as baby flowers, white daisies or heather... to decorate around the mouth of the vase.

So it only takes about 15 minutes and with 5 simple steps you have a beautiful and delicate rose vase to decorate the living room or dining table.

In addition to arranging roses in tall vases in a spherical shape, there are many other flower arrangements, you should learn to be able to make other flower arrangements to diversify flower arrangement recipes, and create New space for the room.

Some notes when arranging roses to stay fresh for a long time

After knowing how to put roses in the vase, there are many women who feel dissatisfied because the flowers do not keep fresh. Especially the rose variety, a very beautiful flower, symbolizing eternal and lasting love. Roses do not last long, but it may be because you have not taken care of them properly. To keep the vase fresh, you need to follow these rules:

Choose a vase

If you want to arrange flowers, you must prepare a suitable vase to arrange a sufficient number, especially the height needs to be balanced with the flower branches.

The bottle needs to be thoroughly cleaned and free from any other chemicals. The substance remaining in the flower needs to be cleaned before planting because it is the cause of the flower stem to rot quickly.

Water plug

If you want fresh flowers, you need to prepare enough water in the vase. Water for flower arrangements needs to be very clean, which will help limit the rotting process of rose branches.

You can use clam broth to keep the roses moist because roses will be freshest when the water has a near-neutral pH. If you use tap water or water left in the refrigerator overnight, there will be chlorine, which will quickly wilt and die. Choose a location to put flowers

The placement of flowers is also very important, contributing to the space of your home, your room add elegance and impression. You should limit the vase of flowers next to the refrigerator, next to the fruit because the substance from fruits and vegetables can absorb all the durability and freshness of flowers.

You should not even leave the vase in a room that is too small or secret. You need to put it in a place with a little air circulation, next to a window or air conditioner vent. You need to place it in a place away from direct sunlight, with a high position, the vase will easily lose water and wither.

Arrange Beautiful Gerbera Flowers

Supplies to prepare

- 5 gold coin flowers
- 3 red gerbera flowers
- 5 pink gerberas
- 3 gerbera pink lotus flowers
- 3 orange gerberas
- Vase, scissors

How to arrange gerbera flowers in a tall vase

Step 1: Wash the flowerpot inside and out, pour water into the jar. Next, you glue the tape to the mouth of the vase to help the flowers stand and distribute evenly.
Step 2: Measure the short length of the flower branches, cut off the leaves and broken, unsightly parts.

Step 3: Stick the light pink and yellow gerbera branches close to the mouth of the vase facing forward. Note: You should plug so that the colors alternate and focus in groups will be more beautiful.

Step 4: Stick the orange and red gerbera branches in a horizontal row behind the short front.

Step 5: You select the yellow and orange gerbera branches behind and adjust it upwards.

Arrange Gerbera Flowers In Low Vases.

Supplies to prepare

- 6 gerbera flowers
- 3 branches of jade chain
- Ganoderma lucidum, slag leaves, flower vases

How to arrange the most beautiful gerbera flower

Step 1: Soak the sponge in water (soak it deep in water) for about 2 minutes and then put it in the vase to make the flower bottom.

Step 2: You separate the leaves at the bottom of the stem of the flower branch and put the decoration in the flower pot to help cover the spongy part. If you plug it with a ceramic vase, there is no need to cover it.

Step 3: Cut off the flower stalk and put it in the middle of the flower pot. The 2nd, 3rd, 4th, 5th, 6th gerbera will be arranged around the side of the top flower so that they are even.

Step 4: You trim the leaves of the jade string and then plug it down the bottom of the flowerpot with the slag leaves to help cover the spongy part and use reishi grass to plug in an arc to make it more vivid.

Arrange Tall Lilies.

If you want to arrange beautiful lilies for a long time, you must first know how to choose beautiful lilies. Choosing a beautiful lily plays an important role in deciding whether Tet lilies can be played for a long time or not. A beautiful lily is a branch of a lily that has many ears (buds), but has not yet bloomed because the lily blooms very quickly.

Ideally, you should choose lily branches with buds that have just arrived so that when you bring them back to arrange the lilies, they will bloom. The flower buds must be big and hard, the leaves are green, the branches are fat and long to be beautiful lilies.

Select materials:

• When arranging lilies, you should remove the anther (or pistil), the lily will last longer, about 2 days longer. In addition, beveled lily branches should be cut so that the flowers can absorb water better. After cutting the bevel, you should soak the lily branches in water for about 5-10 minutes before placing them to keep the flowers fresh longer.

• To keep the lilies fresh for a long time, remember to cut the leaves off the part of the stem that is under the water so that the leaves do not rot in the water, affecting the longevity of the lily.

• A secret to long-lasting, long-lasting lilies that is most often applied by women is to put 1-2 B1 pills, aspirin in a vase of flower arrangement. Mixing 1 liter of flower arrangement with 2 tablespoons of lemon juice also helps lilies stay fresh longer.

• Putting a metal coin in the water to arrange the lilies can also help the flower stem to resist bacteria and prevent rot. You should also change the water for the lilies every 2 days so that the flowers will last longer.

The tall, flared glass lily is a traditional and simple way of arranging lilies, the easiest to do, anyone can arrange lilies this way. For a simple traditional lily arrangement, follow these steps:

Step 1: Prepare a tall, beautiful transparent crystal vase.

Step 2: Choose the longest, most beautiful flower stem as the main lily branch and insert it in the center of the vase. Remember to cut the base of the flower and trim the leaves to make the flower last longer!

Step 3: Plug the next lily branches in descending layers.

Step 4: Insert other leaves and flowers (if you like) to fill the gaps.

Step 5: Adjust the balance between the flower branches so that the lily vase is even.

Arrange White Bayby Flowers Purple Roses.

Ingredient:

- Oasis flower arrangement foam
- Specialized flower wrapping tape
- Cellophane wrapping paper
- Scissors to cut branches
- Foam cutter
- Branch cutter
- Wooden turntable for flowers
- Formex flower box
- White baby flowers
- Purple roses
- Some flowers to decorate your vase (depending on your preference)

Perform

- Firstly, put a layer of cellophane into the flower arrangement box and let it spread out

- Second, put foam in the box to then arrange flowers and then water the sponge to create moisture to help the flowers stay fresh after planting.
long
- Third, fix the foam in the box with specialized flower wrapping tape and then cut the excess flower wrapping paper around the box.

- Fourth, place purple roses on the foam to spread evenly around

- Fifth, arrange white baby flowers interspersed with purple roses

- Sixth, install flowers or decorative branches according to your preferences.

Arrange Lilies

How to choose lilies

You should choose branches that have both buds and flowers open. Such branches when plugged will be beautiful and play for a long time. Buds and flowers must be fresh, do not choose flowers with wilted flowers or crushed branches.

Necessary tools:

Scissors, specialized foam. You can use normal scissors or special scissors to cut flowers more easily. Flower arrangement scissors and foam you can buy on Hang Ma or other stores specializing in flower arrangement accessories. In addition, you can buy more flower conditioners to keep flowers fresh longer.

Choose the right vase

With lilies, you can choose ceramic and porcelain vases if you like the tradition or glass vases if you like a modern and innovative style. Lilies are of the right length, so you should not choose vases or vases that are too tall or too short. How to prepare lilies

After buying flowers, you need to remove the rotten leaves at the base, then wash them, then cut at a 45-degree angle before arranging for the flowers to absorb water better. After cutting, you should soak the flower stems in water for 5-10 minutes.

A vase of lilies for a large living room

If the space of your living room is large, you should choose a porcelain vase that is a little larger in size.

The flower arrangement is very simple. First, you measure the flower with the vase in a ratio of 1:2, meaning the height of the flower spike is twice the height of the vase. Cut the base 45 degrees diagonally, then drop it into the vase. Then remove the leaves on the flower stem and align the flowers so that the flowers are facing out.

To create a focal point for the living room or create inspiration for the office, you can put lilies in the foam and create a round flower shape. To arrange flowers like this, you soak the flower arrangement foam in water so that the foam absorbs the water evenly, place the sponge on top of the flowerpot and then use adhesive tape to fix it.

Cut the lilies short so that from the flower stalk to the cut is only about 5cm, note the cross cut to make it easier to arrange the flowers into the foam. Then slowly insert the lilies into the foam and create a round shape. Use leftover leaves to intersperse into the open styrofoam.

You should change the water once a day to keep the perfume clean and keep the flowers fresh longer. If you do not want to change the water often, you can use a flower conditioner. Lilies usually last for 6 to 10 days.

Plug A Beautiful And Simple Lan

If you want to own a beautiful tabletop orchid pot to display in the party hall, living room, office, etc., don't skip the 5 simple instructions on how to arrange orchids below.

Step 1: Choose a pot to arrange orchids

Choosing the right pot will contribute to the final beauty of the flower pot. Currently, on the market, there are many types of beautiful plug pots, diverse designs. However, no matter which flower pot you choose, you should pay attention to choose a vase that matches the size and color of each type of flower you want to plant to get the most beautiful artistic masterpiece. You should not use pots with colors that are more prominent than flowers or too flashy.

In terms of style, if you want to plant a few flowers, use a small, narrow-mouthed pot or vase. And if you intend to plug the whole root, you should choose a low pot with a wide mouth.

Step 2. Choose the number of flower branches

For those who play feng shui flowers in general and with orchids in particular, choosing the number of flower branches to put in the pot is quite important. Usually, the flower arranger will choose the number of branches such as: 1, 3, 6, 8, 9, 13, 16... In which, 1 means Birth, 3 means Fortune, 6 is Loc, 8 is Phat, number 9 is Truong Cuu, number 13 is Sinh Tai, number 16 is Sinh Loc.

Step 3: Choose flower color

Orchids have many types and each type of orchid will have many different colors. Therefore, depending on your preferences and the meaning you want to convey, you can choose the color according to your needs

Step 4: Choose flower arrangement accessories

Unlike other flowers that need to come with many cumbersome accessories when plugged in, orchids are not too important to this factor because this is a type of natural beauty, the more it is left alone, the more it exudes a proud beauty. sa inherent.

The essential thing you should do is find a standing tree to hold the flower stem in place, for example a piece of foam or coir.... Next is a small iron to bend branches and a little grass to cover the surface of the pot to keep moisture and decorate the flower pot.

Step 5: Shape and arrange flower pots

There are many different ways to arrange flowers, but posing for orchids is indispensable. You can arrange flowers spread in many directions, bend branches or in the same direction to make the orchid pot more vivid and show off.

However, you should be careful and gentle because orchid branches are very brittle and break easily. In addition, you should use nylon threads and strings to lightly tie the flower branches or use candle glue to fix the branches to the iron bar.

Arrange Tulips Simple

Step 1 Before proceeding with the flower arrangement, you need to remove the dead tulip petals. Then, you separate the excess leaves, which are not needed when planting, from the flower.

Step 2 Next, you take the flower stem and measure it with the height of the glass jar that you use to arrange the flowers. Then, you proceed to cut the flower branches so that the length of the branches is 2 times the height of the vase.

Step 3 You put the flower branches together into a bunch and then use an elastic band to tie 1-2 loops outside the stem of the flower branches.

Next, you measure the height of the bouquet you just bouqueted compared to the height of the glass jar again and then adjust the cut and length of the bouquet accordingly.

Step 4 Finally, you pour water into the glass jar first, then proceed to arrange the flowers in the vase so that the bouquet is 3-4cm from the mouth of the vase.

Note:

You should only fill about 2/3 of the glass jar with water because overfilling will cause the water to overflow when you put the flowers in.

Put Hydrangeas In A Vase

Materials to prepare:

- 5 branches of green hydrangea, green leaves
- 1 round vase with diameter 20cm
- Green peel lemon
- 1 round vase with diameter 25cm
- Tools: Knife, cutting board, scissors.

How to arrange hydrangeas:

First, you put the small flowerpot inside the large flowerpot, they will create a slot enough to put the lemon slices in. Accordingly, you slice a lemon about 0.5cm thin, put the slices of lemon in the gap between the two walls of the jar, you continue until the lemon is sealed in the wall.

Finished products:

Create a vase with cool unique lemon slices, you just need to pour water in and arrange flowers. To make the vase beautiful, you should arrange the hydrangeas into a pyramid shape, that is, put the high branches in the center and then arrange the flower branches around with a lower position.

Add small green leaves to make the vase fuller than you have done the hydrangea arrangement.

Instead of plugging into the vase as usual, you add lemon slices to make the vase look cooler. This flower arrangement is not too difficult but anyone can do it.

Put Roses In A Wooden Bowl

Materials to prepare:

• Flowers for arrangement: roses (sister roses, common roses, davit austin roses), small green branches
• 1 small hexagonal net
• 1 wooden bowl
• Tools: Scissors to cut flower branches.

How to arrange roses:

First, you bring out the prepared flowers, trim away the dead, wilted and unnecessary branches. Then, you take the net to cover the mouth of the wooden bowl, this net must be made into many small holes to make sure the flowers are arranged. You just need to bend them to form small holes.

Plug 3 branches of David austin roses close to the mouth of the vase in 3 directions. Plug the branches of roses that are usually lighter in color with sister roses interspersed between 3 branches of David austin roses. Next, put David Austin rose branches straight in the middle of the vase, add green branches interspersed between the flower branches to make it more beautiful.

So you have made a wooden flower bowl with many colors. Leaving flower bowls in the living room will create a highlight to help brighten the house. You can also leave the dining table to serve weekend meals in the family gathering together.

Arrange Beautiful Willow Flowers

If you choose flowers for Tet, you should choose the willow tree that has bloomed beautifully, because the willow flower will keep its shape from the time of purchase until the end, not blooming more or blooming very little. In addition, you do not need to pay attention to the number of branches, but should pay attention to whether the branch has many flowers or not. The more flowers a willow tree has, the more beautiful it will be.

The arrangement of willow flowers is also quite simple. First of all, you need to choose a vase that is suitable for the height of your flower spike. It is best if you arrange flowers for the table, you should buy flower branches about 7 - 80cm high, choose a vase about 30cm is fine. You can use either a ceramic or a glass jar.

Step 1: You wash the flower arrangement with dishwashing liquid and let it dry before you plug it in.

Step 2: Trim the leaves at the bottom of the flower stem and cut the flower stem at a 45-degree angle so that the flower can absorb as much water as possible.

Step 3: Arrange flowers with warm water with a temperature of about 40 - 42 degrees Celsius.

To keep the flowers fresh for a long time during Tet, you can mix in the flower arrangement water a packet of flower balm or a few vitamin B1 tablets, aspirin or lemon juice... In the following days, you should remember to change the water for the flower arrangements regularly. to limit the growth of bacteria as well as to make the flower more durable.

Arrange A Basket Of Yellow Chrysanthemums

Supplies to prepare

• A bouquet of yellow daisies
• A fortune tree
• A flower arrangement
• A small flower basket
• Tools: Blue ribbon, scissors

Doing:

Step 1: Cut the foam to fit the flower basket, soak it in water so that it can absorb evenly and then put it in the flower basket.

Step 2: Cut a chrysanthemum stem about 15cm long and remove the leaves.

Step 3: Stick the chrysanthemum branch in the middle so that the flower faces you.

Step 4: Then, arrange the flower branches to shorten and then arrange them in an arc.

Step 5: Next, arrange the flower branches into a closed, round shape.

Step 6: Plug 3 leaves and the hard part of the leaves into the corner of the flower basket.

The last step: Tie a red ribbon on the handle and you have a lovely flower basket to decorate the corner of the room.

Chrysanthemums In Combination

Materials and tools to prepare:

- 7 branches of yellow chrysanthemums
- 8 branches of gladiolus
- Decorative leaves
- Drag
- Necklace flower vase

Doing:

Step 1: Clean the vase thoroughly with dishwashing liquid to remove all bacteria and dirt. This is also one of the methods to help chrysanthemums stay fresh longer.

Step 2: Mix 2 parts cold water, 1 part hot water to make flower arrangement. To get a flowerpot that is long-lasting and fresh, you can add vitamin B1 or crush aspirin and put it in the jar. Or buy powder packets to help flowers last longer at the store.

Step 3: Estimate the branches of chrysanthemums and gladiolus and then cut them to best fit the height of the vase. When cutting flower stems, it is recommended to cut the bevel at about 45 degrees to increase the contact area with water, helping the flowers absorb water better.

Step 4: Then, arrange the chrysanthemums and gladiolus flowers alternately in a natural way.

Step 5: Plug in more decorative leaves around the vase to make the colors more harmonious and vivid.

Chrysanthemums With Tea Cups

Besides the old tea pot, with just a pair of tea cups, you can also become a talented creator with an artistic vase of chrysanthemums.

Supplies to prepare

- A pair of tea cups and plates
- 3 branches of white and yellow fake daisies with flowers and leaves.
- Tools: Hard wire with white plastic coating, glue gun, pliers, scissors

Doing:

Step 1: Cut a piece of zinc wire from 18 cm to 20 cm long, divide the zinc section into 3 folded parts. The first part of the zinc wire is fixed to the disc, the other end is fixed to the wall of the cup opposite the handle position. Let the handle of the tea cup face up, the middle is the height of the falling flower waterfall.

Step 2: Cut short the calyx of chrysanthemums, branches and pistils to make flower waterfalls. Use a glue gun to glue the branches and leaves to the center of the bottom of the cup and then glue 2 daisies on both sides, try to create a perfect shape before gluing it in place with tape.

Step 3: Paste the yellow flowers alternating with white chrysanthemums, note, and paste so that the flowers in the cup face the outside.

Step 4: Cleverly glue the white chrysanthemum flowers behind the waterfall to cover the zinc part. Finally, glue the flowers to the plate to finish. To be more perfect, you can add butterfly wings, other small decorative items next to the flower waterfall.

Chrysanthemums On Moss Tray

Supplies to prepare

- 7 small white daisies,
- 7 violets (choose the same size)
- 1 transparent glass dish
- Fresh moss with a bit of soil clinging to it.
- Tools: 1 water bottle and flower scissors

Doing:

Step 1: Cover the surface of the dish with moss evenly, allowing the soil to stick to the moss to stay fresh longer. It is recommended to add a few slices of foam to keep the moss fresh longer and to use it for flower arrangements.

Step 2: Cut chrysanthemum stalks about 4cm long depending on how thick or thin your moss layer is.

Step 3: Plug 7 chrysanthemums spread evenly on the plate, flower stalks are deeply submerged in moss or foam.

Step 4: Insert violets alternately with white daisies. Then sprinkle the water evenly. You can also use a mist sprayer to lightly coat the plate with flowers and moss, which will add a beautiful and long-lasting look.

Arrange Cat Tuong Flowers

Prepare:

4 branches of auspicious flowers, 3 branches of orchid and 4 palm leaves, 1 washed crystal or glass vase, 1 pair of scissors for pruning flowers and leaves.

How to arrange flowers:

Put about 2/3 of clean water dissolved with 1 aspirin or 2 tablespoons of lemon juice into the jar. The purpose is to keep the flowers fresh for a long time and disinfect the water during the flower arrangement. At the same time, prevent flowers from root rot affecting the freshness of flowers during the display process.

Prune 1 flower stem as desired so that the height of the flower branch is ⅔ the height of the vase. The next flower branches, pay attention to prune the next flower branch lower than the previous flower branch and arrange for them to spread evenly along the mouth of the vase. Pay attention to choose healthy auspicious flowers that have both flowers and buds and do not choose flowers that are already in full bloom.

To make the vase as auspicious as more natural and shimmering, use palm leaves to add more points to the mouth of the jar. This step can both cover the mouth of the vase and bring a natural and elegant look to the vase.

Finally, add more orchid leaves and adjust them to fit the eyes so that the vase becomes more graceful and natural.

Arrange Sunflowers

The simplest and most beautiful way to arrange flower sunflowers is to put the whole branches in a tall vase. This is a way of arranging sunflowers that almost anyone can do if they follow the instructions properly.

Here, in this article, we will show you how to put sunflowers in a glass vase for the most beautiful!

Prepare

- 10 branches of sunflowers.
- 15 sprigs of primrose or baby.
- 1 branch of orchid leaves.
- 8 fern leaves.
- Tall glass vase.
- Scissors cut flower branches, adhesive tape in small version.

Doing:

Step 1: Fill the vase with water 2/3, then use adhesive tape to stick it on the mouth of the vase, divide the mouth of the vase into cells so that the flower arrangement stands firm and evenly distributed.

Since the sunflower stem is quite heavy, you can add pebbles to the water to make the flower pot stand.

Step 2: Before arranging flowers, you need to cut off all the leaves on the stem of the flower and cut the branches so that the height is just right compared to the vase.

When cutting the flower base, you should cut the beveled shape so that the flower base can absorb water better, helping the flower stay fresh longer!

Step 3: Choose the largest and most beautiful sunflower and place it in the center of the vase. Then arrange another flower around so that the flowers spread evenly on all 4 sides.

You just need to arrange each sunflower branch according to the rule of crisscrossing each other, one flower will not be obscured by the other.

Step 4: Insert cycads, a few small fern branches into other open areas to cover the gaps and make the vase more attractive and eye-catching.

Arrange Lavender

Lavender is a rustic flower, so it can be planted alone or combined with small flowers, wheat flowers with a sense of home. The flowerpot should also be a small vase with a delicate and unique vintage look. In this article, I will guide you to arrange dried lavender lavender along with other small dried flowers to create accents.

Prepare:

- Dried lavender
- Dried flowers, chrysanthemums
- Small coil of rope or ribbon

How to bouquet lavender

Step 1: Arrange lavender alternately / next to other small flowers based on your preferences and senses.

Step 2: Wrap the string around the flower branch to fix the bouquet shape. Can be wrapped short or high to form small bouquets.

Step 3: Plug the bouquet into the bottle, jar and can tie a bow to increase the lovely and lively feature. These lavender bouquets can also be placed in each small room, drawer to help decorate, scent the room or give to friends and relatives.

Note when planting lavender:

Fresh lavender should be bundled into small bunches and hung in a ventilated area to dry naturally. Dried lavender retains its fragrance, color and lasts longer.

Dried lavender needs to be carefully preserved on rainy, humid days. Put them in a zip bag, tightly tied nylon bag to avoid moldy flowers.

Do not put dried lavender in small mouth vases, vertical vases and tall vases because moisture can collect in the vases and cause the flowers to become moldy.

Should choose a wide-mouth, low vase or bamboo and rattan baskets to plant dried lavender and preserve flowers better.

Arrange Round Peonies

If you are wondering how to arrange a beautiful and delicate peony, do not worry because the round design is not too difficult to do. This formula applies to both low and high pitchers.

Materials to prepare:

- Custom peonies
- Adhesive tape or lanyard
- Scissors
- Vase of flowers

Steps to arrange round peonies:

Step 1: First, prepare the peonies according to the suggestions above. Then fill with water ½ or 1/3 of the height of the pitcher.

Step 2: Then, you cross the flower stem clockwise. Just place each flower spike in your hand and stack them on top of each other so that the flower head forms a round block. Next, use adhesive tape or string to fix the flower more firmly. Or don't like to be fixed but let it be natural.

Step 3: You cut the flower base 45 degrees to make the flowers even. Then put it in the vase and you're done.

*Note how to arrange peonies with vases:

If you like to arrange a lot of flowers, you should choose a tall and wide vase. And if you only plug about 5.7 flowers, you can choose a low, small vase.

With a short vase, you cut the flower close to the mouth of the vase. For tall vases, cut at a ratio of about 1: 1.5, which means that the flower is 1.5 times taller than the vase.

Arrange Peonies With Other Flowers

If you like to have more colors and be as creative as you like, then learn how to arrange peonies with other flowers below. It's not difficult at all, but it's also very interesting.

Materials to prepare:

- Peony
- Flowers, other leaves for decoration
- Foam
- Flowerpot or square box, rectangular box
- Scissors

Steps to arrange peonies with other flowers:

Step 1: First, you prepare the peony with other flowers and leaves. Fill about ½ or 1/3 of the vase with water.

Step 2: Next, put the biggest and brightest peony in the middle. The secondary flowers are interwoven lower in the surrounding position. Interweave leaves in the gap to cover the foam if used as a finishing touch

Note how to arrange peonies with other flowers:

You can combine peony with leaves or flowers of smaller size, for example, roses, willow flowers, baby flowers, ... – Peonies have many different colors such as white, pink pale, ... but should only choose 1-2 colors together. Choosing too many colors makes the whole look messy.

If you want the peony to bloom quickly, you should place the vase in a well-lit place or near a light. You should change the water once a day to keep the perfume clean and keep the flowers fresh longer. If you do not want to change the water often, you can use a flower conditioner.

Because peonies are imported flowers, you should choose to buy flowers at reputable stores

With beautiful flowers like peonies, don't ignore the ways to arrange peonies above. Make sure guests coming to the house to play will love it.

Made in United States
North Haven, CT
28 May 2024

53042452R00078